CONTENTS

WELCOME TO THE WORLD OF INFOGRAPHICS

Using icons, graphics and pictograms, infographics visualise data and information in a whole new way!

WEIGH THE AMOUNT OF KRILL A BLUE WHALE CAN EAT IN CARS

SEE HOW MANY OFFSPRING A GARDEN SNAIL CAN HAVE IN A YEAR

MEASURE THE HEIGHT OF THE WORLD'S TALLEST TERMITE MOUND

BE AMAZED BY THE ANIMAL KINGDOM'S LARGEST EYE

WHAT IS AN ANIMAL?

Animals are living organisms that feed on other organisms and react to the world using their senses. Found all over the world, they range in size from tiny microscopic creatures to the enormous blue whale.

THE ANIMAL KINGDOM CAN BE DIVIDED INTO TWO GROUPS:

Invertebrates
animals without backbones

Invertebrates make up
95–99 per cent
of Earth's animal species.

Vertebrates
animals with backbones

MOVEMENT

While some animals live in one place, most move around in search of food and places to breed. Canada geese can cover **2,400 km in just 24 hours** when they migrate…

... while a leatherback turtle was recorded travelling 20,558 km in 647 days.

That is the same as travelling half-way around the globe.

COMPOUND EYE

RESPOND TO THE WORLD

Animals have special body parts that help them sense the outside world. These include eyes, ears and antennae. Insects have special compound eyes that are made up of thousands of individual units. Some animals have evolved ways of communicating, telling others about the information they have gathered.

DIRECTION OF FOOD SOURCE

LOOP 2

LOOP 1

Dragonflies have as many as **30,000** lenses in each eye.

Bees perform a **loop dance** to show others in the hive where food can be found.

EATING FOOD

Unlike plants, which can make their food using energy from the Sun, animals need to eat other living things to survive.

An adult blue whale can eat about **3.5 tonnes of krill** in a single day.

That is the same weight as three small cars.

Pythons have been recorded eating prey that is more than **50 per cent** of their own body weight.

CLASSIFYING ANIMALS

Scientists divide living things into groups that share the same characteristics. These groups are further divided into sub-groups, the smallest being the individual species.

KINGDOMS

The biggest groups are the kingdoms; most scientists divide the living world into **six kingdoms.** The kingdoms are divided into more and more precise sub-groups based on shared characteristics.

ANIMALS

PLANTS

FUNGI

PROTISTS
(MICRO-ORGANISMS)

EUBACTERIA
(MICRO-ORGANISMS)

ARCHEOBACTERIA
(MICRO-ORGANISMS)

PHYLUM: *CHORDATA*
Kingdoms are divided into phyla. *Chordata* are animals that have a spinal cord.

CLASS: *MAMMALIA*
A phylum is divided into classes. Mammals are animals with hair and produce milk.

ORDER: *CARNIVORA*
A class is divided into orders. Carnivores are animals that can eat meat.

FAMILY: *FELIDAE*
An order is divided into families. Felidae is the family that includes the big cats.

GENUS: *PANTHERA*
A family is divided into genera (single: genus). Panthera includes four living species.

SPECIES: *TIGER, LION, LEOPARD, JAGUAR*
A genus is divided into different species.

HOW MANY
ANIMAL SPECIES?

Scientists have described more than **1.5 million animal species, including...**

MOTHS AND BUTTERFLIES
160,000
SPECIES

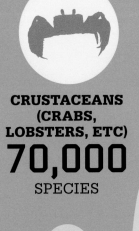

CRUSTACEANS (CRABS, LOBSTERS, ETC)
70,000
SPECIES

FISH
32,000
SPECIES

MAMMALS
6,000
SPECIES

BEETLES
400,000
SPECIES

However, it is estimated that there are around **9–10 million animal species.**

EATING AND ENERGY

The Sun is the source of most of the energy used on our planet. Plants convert this energy into substances that living things can then use to produce energy to survive and grow.

Primary consumers

Animals that eat plants are called primary consumers. They have special body adaptations to get the nutrients from plants.

A giraffe has a tongue that measures up to

50 CM

long, which it uses to grasp and pull leaves and branches off trees.

A ruminant, such as a cow, has a special stomach. This partially digests plant food, before it is regurgitated, **chewed again and swallowed**.

4. The partially digested food, now called cud, is regurgitated and chewed again.

1. Ruminant chews plant food before swallowing it.

5. The cud is swallowed into another part of the stomach, before going through the rest of the guts.

3. The food enters the next stomach compartment, the reticulum.

2. The chewed food enters the first compartment of the stomach, called the rumen.

Secondary consumers

Also known as predators, these creatures eat other animals. They have **keen senses** and **special adaptations** to hunt and catch their prey.

HEAT-SENSITIVE PITS

Some snakes use special heat-sensitive pits to hunt for prey. These pits can detect temperature variations in their surroundings of just 0.2°C.

Sperm whales will dive to depths of around,

1,000 M

holding their breath for up to **90 minutes** while hunting for fish and squid.

Great white sharks can detect **a drop of blood** in 100 litres of water

THAT IS MORE THAN TWICE THE HEIGHT OF THE EMPIRE STATE BUILDING

443.2M

Recyclers

These creatures feed on waste and the remains of dead things.

One hectare of soil can contain **500,000 earthworms.** Together, they can eat **9 tonnes** of leaves, stems and dead roots a year (equivalent in weight to two elephants).

Earthworms range in length from **1 mm to 3 metres.**

MAMMALS

Mammals can regulate their body heat. They have bodies that are covered with hair and they feed their young on milk. Most of them give birth to live young.

YOUNG

The young of most mammals develop inside the body of the mother. This time is called the gestation period and varies from species to species.

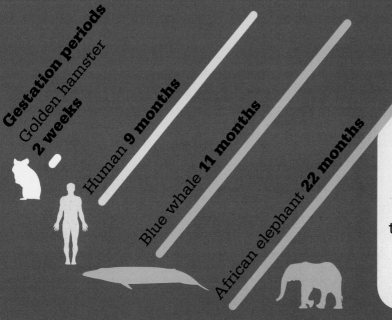

Gestation periods

Golden hamster **2 weeks**

Human **9 months**

Blue whale **11 months**

African elephant **22 months**

The **largest newborn mammal** belongs to the **blue whale** – it weighs about **2.7 tonnes** at birth.

Three mammal species, all found in Australasia, lay eggs instead of giving birth to live young. They are called **monotremes** and include two species of **echidna**, also known as spiny anteaters, as well as the **platypus.**

ACTUAL SIZE

A platypus egg is about the size of a thumbnail. It hatches around 10 days after being laid.

The bill-like snout has special sensors to detect prey hiding in the mud of riverbeds.

A male platypus has venomous spurs on its back legs.

MILK PRODUCTION

The make-up of mammal milk varies, depending on where the animal lives and how fast the young need to grow. For example, some mammals live in cold regions and need thick layers of insulation, so their milk is very rich in fats.

- sugars
- proteins
- fats
- water

Human milk

- sugars
- proteins — 70
- fats — 15
- — 40
- water — 870

ml/mg per litre

Cow milk

- sugars
- proteins — 44
- fats — 33
- — 34
- water — 880

ml/mg per litre

Reindeer milk

- sugars
- proteins
- fats — 28
- — 109
- — 171
- water — 677

ml/mg per litre

smallest and largest

ACTUAL SIZE

Kitti's hog-nosed bat
30–40 mm, 1.5–2 g

← 22.5 m →

Blue whale
20–30 metres,
100–160 tonnes

MAMMAL BRAINS

Mammals usually have bigger brains than other animals of the same size.

Sperm whales have the largest brain of any living animal.

8,000 cubic cm

1,300 cubic cm

REPTILES

There are more than 9,400 species of reptile and they live on every continent, except for Antarctica. While most have four legs, some, including snakes, have no legs and slither over the ground.

Reptile characteristics

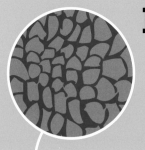

They have scales covering their bodies.

Reptiles have backbones.

They breathe air using lungs.

Most lay eggs with leathery shells.

Almost all of them are cold-blooded.

Leatherback turtles can control their body heat to a certain degree, to cope with diving into deep, icy water.

Because reptiles do not need energy to keep their **body temperature** constant, they only need to eat **2–3%** of the amount mammals and birds of similar sizes eat.

Saltwater crocodiles can lay more than 60 eggs inside a single nest.

HOW SNAKES MOVE

Snakes use different methods of pushing their bodies along the ground.

CONCERTINA

SERPENTINE

SIDEWINDING

Giant reptiles

The Komodo dragon, the world's biggest lizard, can grow to **3 metres long** and weigh **135 kg**.

The record for a leatherback turtle is **2.6 m long** and a weight of **916 kg**.

The largest living reptile is the **saltwater crocodile**, which can grow to **7 metres long** and weigh **1,000 kg...**

...as much as a small car.

AMPHIBIANS

There are about 6,500 species of amphibians found in the world. These animals cannot control their own body heat and are known as cold-blooded. They rely on the Sun to warm them up.

AMPHIBIANS WORLDWIDE

Amphibians spend their lives both in water and on dry land, and are found on every continent apart from Antarctica.

■ Inhabited by amphibians

They have no .... scales and their skin is permeable.

Many amphibians, such as this newt, can actually 'breathe' through their skin. As a result they lose a lot of water through their skin as well, and must spend a lot of time in water or moist places.

Amphibian metamorphosis

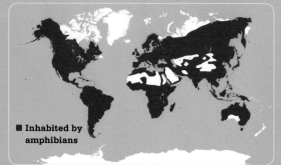

Day 112:
Adult frog

Day 1: Eggs

Day 6:
Tadpole

LIFE CYCLE OF A FROG

Frogs develop from eggs, or frog spawn, into tadpoles, before changing into adult frogs.

Day 84:
Froglet

The **spring peeper** frog can survive the winter with **65 per cent** of its body water **frozen as ice.**

The toxins from one poison dart frog, *Phyllobates terribilis*, could kill more than

90
people.

Wallace's flying frog can glide for 15 metres or more from tree to tree (or to the ground) in search of prey or when escaping from a predator.

school bus

<···················· **13 m** ····················>

Smallest and biggest

ACTUAL SIZE

The smallest frog in the world is found in Papua New Guinea and measures about 7.5 mm long when fully grown.

Japanese salamanders are some of the biggest amphibians in the world. They can grow to a length of 1.5 m and weigh up to **25 kg**. The biggest amphibians are **Chinese salamanders**, which can reach

1.8 m long.

BIRDS

There are more than 9,500 species of bird and they all have wings, lay eggs and have bodies that are covered with feathers. They either live in huge flocks or as solitary hunters with razor-sharp beaks and claws.

WINGS
The shape of a bird's wings depends on the type of flying it does – whether it is soaring or zig-zagging in short bursts.

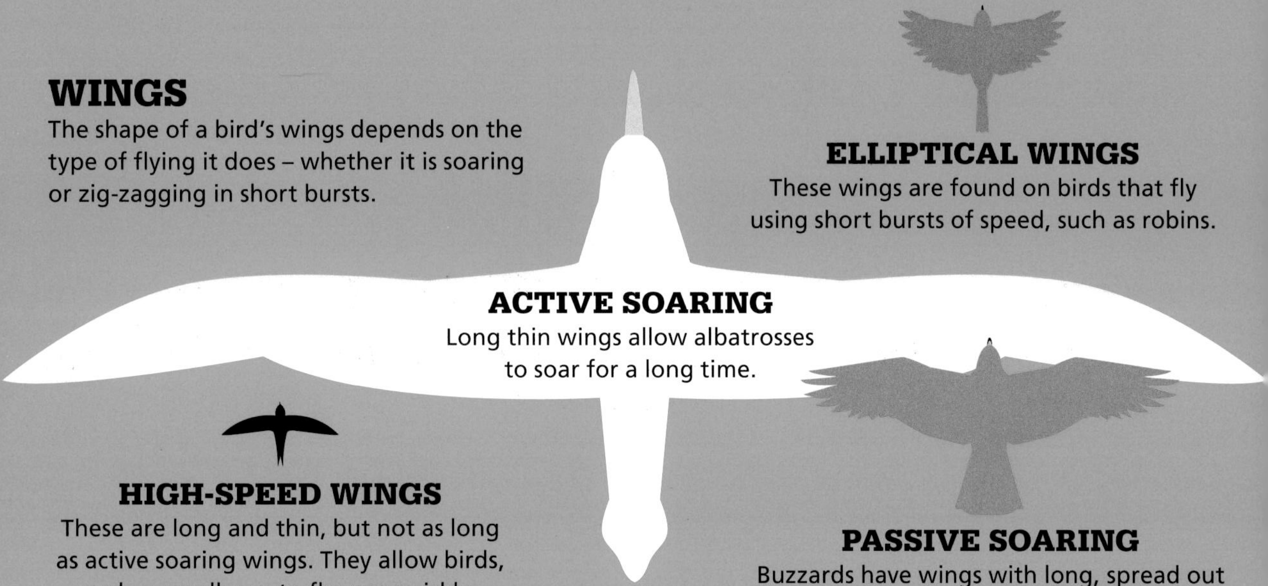

ELLIPTICAL WINGS
These wings are found on birds that fly using short bursts of speed, such as robins.

ACTIVE SOARING
Long thin wings allow albatrosses to soar for a long time.

HIGH-SPEED WINGS
These are long and thin, but not as long as active soaring wings. They allow birds, such as swallows, to fly very quickly.

PASSIVE SOARING
Buzzards have wings with long, spread out feathers, which they use to catch rising currents of warm air, called thermals.

TALONS
The most powerful bird of prey, the harpy eagle, has a wingspan of around 2 m. Its talons, shown here at actual size, can be up to 12.5 cm long.

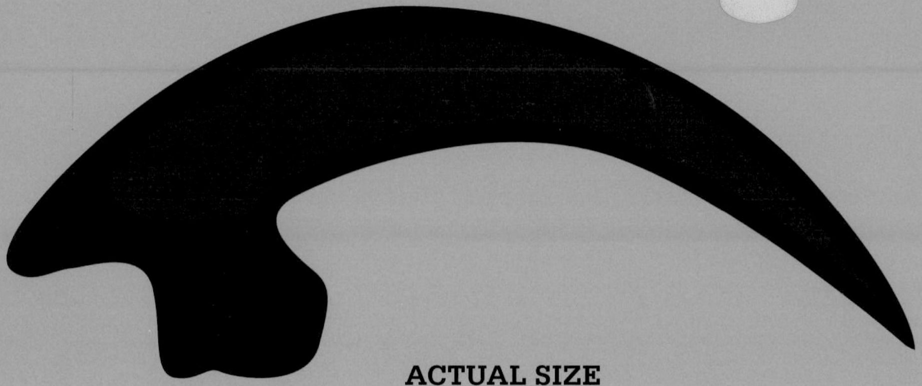

FEATHERS
All birds have feathers. They are used for insulation, to aid flying and to create amazing patterns, which birds use for display.

ACTUAL SIZE

20 mins

DIVING BIRDS

Emperor penguins can dive down to depths of **565 metres** (deeper than any other bird) and stay underwater for 20 minutes.

1,500,000,000

the number of **red-billed quelea** in Africa.

They form huge flocks that can take five hours to pass overhead.

LAYING EGGS

The kiwi lays the largest eggs relative to the size of its body. One female weighing 1.7 kg laid an egg weighing 0.4 kg.

The smallest bird egg was laid by a German crested canary. It measured just 7 mm long and weighed less than 0.03 g.

ACTUAL SIZE

SMALLEST EGG

The tail of a **peacock** measures about **1.5 metres**, making up about **60%** of the bird's entire length.

FISH

There are more than 30,000 species of fish living in the salty waters of the seas and oceans and the freshwater of rivers and lakes.

Fish characteristics

They live in water.

Almost all fish are cold-blooded.

... They breathe using gills.

They have a backbone.

They swim using fins. ....

Most of them have scales.

HOW GILLS WORK

Fish use organs called gills to take oxygen out of the water.

Blood vessels.

Gill filaments.

1. Water, shown in white, flows in through the mouth and over the gills.

<........ Flow of water

2. As water flows over the gills, oxygen passes from the water into the blood flowing through the thin gill filaments.

Archer fish hunt by spitting a stream of water at insects above the water surface. This knocks them into the water.

They can hit prey up to **1.2 metres** away – the equivalent of a human spitting at a target more than 19 metres away.

Flying fish can glide for up to **200 metres** above the water's surface – the length of two football pitches.

← -- →
200 m

Record fish

Supported by water, some fish have evolved to gigantic sizes.

MOUNT EVEREST
8,848 METRES HIGH

The deepest-living fish, **_Abyssobrotula galathea_**, was found living in a trench at the bottom of the Atlantic Ocean, some 8,370 m below the surface – almost the height of Mt Everest (8,848 m).

The world's smallest fish, _Paedocypris progenetica_, can be just **7.9 mm** long when fully grown.

ACTUAL SIZE

The biggest fish is the **whale shark.** The largest measured specimen was **12.65 m long**.

It weighed **21 tonnes...** ... about the same as **4 elephants.**

BUGS

Insects and arachnids are part of a group of animals called arthropods. These creatures are invertebrates and are covered in hard outer skeletons called exoskeletons.

Insects and arachnids

Insects and arachnids look **similar**, but there are key differences between the two animal **classes**.

Insects have three body parts (head, thorax and abdomen) and six legs.

Arachnids have just two body parts (cephalothorax and abdomen), but eight legs.

Head

Two antennae

Six legs

Six pairs of appendages

Thorax

Abdomen

Cephalothorax

Eight legs

80%

There are more species of insect than any other animal group – they make up 80 per cent of the world's arthropod species.

Insects are some of the most common living things on the planet. There are

800,000-900,000 species of insect.

Ceratopogonidae, or biting midges, can flap their wings around

1,050 times per second.

San Lorenzo forest, Panama

Many insects live in huge, hierarchical colonies.

Scientists have found as many as **25,000** species of insect living in the **6,000 hectare** San Lorenzo forest in Panama,

AN AREA SMALLER THAN MANHATTAN, NEW YORK

8,746 hectares

A termite queen can lay up to **7,000 eggs** a day, and may live for **50 years.**

A termite colony can have as many as **3,000,000** insects, including young, workers, soldiers and at least one queen.

The largest termite mound discovered measured **12.8 metres tall.**

Scientists have found webs of the Darwin's bark spider in Madagascar that are **25 metres wide** – as long as two city buses.

22.5 m

HARD SHELLS

Many creatures use a tough outer shell to support and protect their bodies. Even with these rigid body parts, some animals with hard shells can grow to be as big as a small car.

Types of shell

Turtle
The shell comes in two halves: the carapace on the top and the plastron on the bottom.

Crabs
As crabs grow, they continually shed and re-grow their shells, too.

Snails
A snail's shell grows along with the animal.

120,000,000

The number of red crabs estimated to live on Christmas Island – 60,000 times more than the human population, which numbers just over 2,000.

ACTUAL SIZE

The largest millipede in the world is the **African giant black millipede**

The **Japanese spider crab** can measure **3.7 m** from the tip of one claw to the other, but their bodies only measure 35 cm across.

Just 30 cm long, the **mantis shrimp** uses a fast punch to disable prey.

Giant clams can grow to 1.2 metres across and weigh more than 225 kg – that is the weight of about **three adult humans**.

It hits with the force of a **.22 calibre bullet**, smashing through any protective shell.

1.2 m

A SINGLE GARDEN SNAIL CAN HAVE **430** OFFSPRING IN A YEAR.

which can grow to nearly **40 cm long.**

SOFT BODIES

Thousands of animal species do not have a skeleton of any kind, internal or external. Instead, their bodies are soft, allowing them to squeeze through tiny gaps, or if they are supported by water, to grow to enormous sizes.

Squid are the fastest marine invertebrates. They squeeze out a jet of water to push them forwards at speeds of up to

40 km/h

– faster than an Olympic sprinter at 37.5 km/h.

Some slugs can stretch their bodies to more than **10 times** their original length to squeeze through tiny spaces.

BURJ KHALIFA, 829.84 M

1,000 M

Sea cucumbers live on the ocean floor at depths ranging from 500 m to 5,000 m. They can swim **1,000 m** up from the sea floor while hunting for food – **higher than the world's tallest building to date, the Burj Khalifa, Dubai.**

stretching far out into the ocean, the lion's mane jellyfish is one of the world's longest creatures. The longest specimen ever found measured 37 m – longer than a blue whale.

Giant Pacific octopuses can grow to more than **9 metres** across and weigh up to **270 kg...**

... but this is dwarfed by the monster of the deep, the giant squid, which can grow to **18 metres long** and weigh **900 kg.**

37 M

20-30 M

Living between **600 m** and **900 m** below the surface, the giant squid is longer than the world's biggest fish and even most whales.

ACTUAL SIZE

Giant squid have the largest eyes on the planet – up to

25 cm
in diameter

MOVERS AND SHAKERS

Some animals travel thousands of kilometres searching for water, food or the right place to raise their young. These long journeys are called migrations.

MIGRATIONS
Comparison of some of the longest migrations:

NORTH AMERICA

EUROPE

AFRICA

SOUTH AMERICA

ANTARCTICA

Every autumn, **monarch butterflies** leave their home range in Canada and the US and migrate some **3,200 km** to southern California and Mexico.

Each year, on Africa's Serengeti Plains, more than **1.5 million** wildebeest migrate in search of food. They are preyed upon by 3,000 lions.

Swarms of locusts migrate from one area when food becomes scarce. These swarms can number

10,000,000,000

and cover an area of **1,000 sq km,** around the size of Berlin, Germany's capital city.

ASIA

AUSTRALIA

European eels reproduce in the Sargasso Sea (western Atlantic and Caribbean). When the eggs hatch, the young are carried by ocean currents back to Europe, where they swim up rivers to grow and mature for up to 20 years. When fully grown they make the return trip to the Sargasso Sea to reproduce, a trip of **5,000–7,000 km** each way.

Some **leatherback turtles** migrate **6,000 km** each way between feeding and breeding areas.

Arctic terns make a round-trip of **44,000 km** from the Arctic to Antarctica and back every year.

ENDANGERED AND EXTINCT

Animal species are threatened by many natural causes. But thousands of species are threatened today by the actions of humans, through hunting or habitat destruction.

90%

More than 90% of all the organisms that have ever lived on Earth are extinct.

Possible causes of extinction events:

Gradual change in environment (cooling or warming)

Cataclysmic event: volcanic eruption or meteorite collision

Human activity

Mass extinction events

The **Permian mass extinction** about **250 million years ago** saw **96 per cent** of species die out, possibly because of an asteroid impact, volcanic eruptions or a drop in oxygen level – or a combination of these.

96%

..... survived

32.4% threatened

Of the 6,260 amphibian species listed by the IUCN (International Union for the Conservation of Nature), nearly one-third (2,030 species) are extinct or threatened.

Whaling

Blue whales are currently at one per cent of their original numbers.

1% ......>⊖

Humpback whales

Scientific estimates put the number of humpback whales at 1.5 million before the start of commercial whaling in the 1800s. Today, they number just

20,000

Habitat destruction

Because the forests they live in are being destroyed, scientists estimate that there are just **1,300 pandas left** in the wild. That is one panda for every 5.4 million people.

Hunting

The dodo was a flightless bird that lived on the island of Mauritius. It was first seen in 1507. Due to hunting and the introduction of predators, it was extinct by 1681.

GLOSSARY

adaptation
A characteristic of an animal that has come about through evolution and which gives the animal an advantage in its environment.

characteristic
A feature or quality of an animal.

cold-blooded
Unlike warm-blooded animals, cold-blooded animals cannot regulate their own temperature, but rely on the heat of the Sun to warm them up. Cold-blooded animals are often slow-moving in cold weather.

evolved
Something that has changed over time – all animal species gradually change and adapt to their environments.

exoskeleton
A hard, protective outer covering that some invertebrates have.

extinct
Something that has died out and no longer exists.

gestation
The period between an egg being fertilised and the young being born, also known as pregnancy.

gills
The breathing organs of fish and some other aquatic animals, which extract oxygen from the water.

habitat
The environment in which an organism lives.

hierarchical
A group of things that is arranged in order of importance. A hierarchical colony or society has the most important individuals at the top and the least important at the bottom.

invertebrate
An animal that does not have a backbone.

metamorphosis
When an organism's body undergoes a major change as it gets older. For example, a frog starts out as a tadpole with a tail and gills, before later changing into a tailless adult frog with lungs.

migrate
To move to a new area, usually in search of food, water, partners to mate with, or a suitable place to raise young.

micro-organism
A living creature that is too small to be seen with the naked eye.

species
A group of organisms that share the same physical characteristics and are capable of breeding with one another.

thermal
A rising current of warm air.

monotreme
A rare type of mammal that lays eggs rather than giving birth to live young.

vertebrate
An animal that has a backbone.

warm-blooded
Warm-blooded animals can control their own body temperature and do not need to rely on the heat of the Sun.

organism
An individual form of life, such as an animal, a plant or a fungus.

permeable
A permeable skin or membrane is one that allows gas or fluids to pass through it.

senses
The ways in which animals gather information about the the outside world. This includes sight, hearing, smell, taste and touch, as well as several other senses.

Websites

MORE INFO:
http://www.zsl.org/kids/
The kids' section of the Zoological Society of London's website is packed with animal information, games and activites, as well as the latest scientific studies on animal life.

kids.nationalgeographic.com/kids/animals/
Animal-related facts, pictures and games from the kids' section of the National Geographic website.

www.nhm.ac.uk/kids-only
The Natural History Museum website is filled with games, facts and information on the world of animals, both living and extinct.

MORE GRAPHICS:
www.visualinformation.info
A website that contains a whole host of infographic material on subjects as diverse as natural history, science, sport and computer games.

www.coolinfographics.com
A collection of infographics and data visualisations from other online resources, magazines and newspapers.

www.dailyinfographic.com
A comprehensive collection of infographics on an enormous range of topics that is updated every single day!

INDEX

ACKNOWLEDGEMENTS

Published in paperback in 2014 by Wayland
Copyright © Wayland 2014

Wayland
338 Euston Road
London NW1 3BH

Wayland Australia
Level 17/207 Kent Street
Sydney NSW 2000

All rights reserved.
Senior editor: Julia Adams

Produced by Tall Tree Ltd
Editors: Jon Richards and Joe Fullman
Designers: Ed Simkins and Ben Ruocco
Consultant: Kim Bryan

Dewey classification: 590

ISBN: 9780750283199

10 9 8 7 6 5 4 3 2 1

Printed in China

Wayland is a division of Hachette
Children's Books, an Hachette UK company.
www.hachette.co.uk

The website addresses (URLs) included in this
book were valid at the time of going to press.
However, because of the nature of the Internet,
it is possible that some addresses may have
changed, or sites may have changed or closed
down, since publication. While the author and
Publisher regret any inconvenience this may
cause the readers, no responsibility for any such
changes can be accepted by either the author
or the Publisher.